get out of your way

RUSS

HARPER
DESIGN

An Imprint of HarperCollinsPublishers

HarperCollins books may be purchased for educational, business,
or sales promotional use. For information, please email the
Special Markets Department at SPsales@harpercollins.com.

"Humble" from THE AMERICAN HERITAGE DICTIONARY,
Fifth Edition, Copyright © 2012 by Houghton Mifflin Harcourt
Publishing Company. Reprinted by permission of Houghton
Mifflin Harcourt Publishing Company. All rights reserved.

FIRST EDITION
Design by Adam Foda
Layout by Tanya Ross-Hughes

Library of Congress Control Number: 2019036429
ISBN 978-0-06-296243-0

Printed in the United States of America.

21 22 23 LSC   10 9

I dedicate this book to you.

CONTENTS

YOU ARE HERE.

If you have a dream, read this book. If you're flipping through these pages you probably have a little flame flickering, waiting for you to pour gas on it—something you want to do, to be, to make. There is nothing that's impossible.

Music is the lens through which I see the world. I express my truth through my music. Music is one of the most pure examples of a higher power. You can't touch music. It's a feeling. Music is the soul stripped away from the body, in audio format. When you record music, you transcend your body. It is an example of manifesting—bringing something into existence using what's in your head.

Making music teaches me so much about myself and the world. But it isn't music itself that teaches me, it is the pursuit of my greatest passion. Whatever that thing is that takes you to a higher level, that connects you to the best possible version of yourself, that helps you live purposefully—THAT'S YOUR PASSION.

But my success actually has very little to do with the music. I'm simply a vessel that communicates my higher purpose. Connecting to your higher purpose is essential. All the tools I used to create my success in music is easily applicable to just about anything you are passionate about, whether it is starting a business or following an artistic calling or strengthening a community. But passion and self-belief are paramount to any endeavor. Your success is directly related to your self-belief. I couldn't even get to the point where I could make a song that you love if I was not mentally equipped to go through ten years of sounding terrible. Sure, now the song sounds good, but that took years, not just of practice but of delusional self-belief. It was a long process of anonymity, putting out songs that no one heard—and the whole time maintaining an unwavering belief that on any given day I could wake up and discover that my music had blown up.

There are three essential qualities required for turning your real life into your dream life: delusion, persistence, and gratitude.

Delusion will give you faith when there is absolutely nothing in your present life that indicates you should believe. It is ABSOLUTELY all in your head.

Persistence will provide strength to keep going.

Gratitude allows you to appreciate all that you have and the achievement of your goals, both small and large. *What you think about, you bring about.* The positive energy generated by your gratitude will yield more blessings, and you will see that your dream will continually unfold.

Get out of your way.

As far back as I can remember, I've always had pure, undiluted confidence. I was confident in myself before I even knew myself. In high school, before

I'd turn in a test, I'd write "100%" at the top of the page. (Yeah, my teachers were not fond of me. I was voted "Most Likely to Make a Teacher Retire." But I always made really good grades.) When I was fourteen, I started making beats. Although now I can tell you objectively that they were terrible, back then I thought they were the most amazing beats ever. Even as a little kid I was obsessed with being the best. At five years old, playing basketball with my brother, I was a veteran shit-talker. I have always had this stain of confidence, even when I didn't really know what I was being confident in.

I know it sounds nutty, but I genuinely believe, with every ounce of my body, that I have never failed. You could say putting out eleven projects and none of them blowing up was a failure, but I don't look at it like that. Where you see failure, I see stepping stones.

To win, you need to get out of your own way. You decide whether to be your greatest obstacle or your biggest fan. The secret is being able to ride out the time between when you're the only one who believes that what is in your head is actually going to come to fruition, and the moment when it actually does. That period is when everything can go left. It can make the most confident mind doubtful. That's where you lose. You don't lose to a competitor or to an industry or to a boss—you lose to yourself. Defeating your own self-doubt is the biggest obstacle to overcome.

At seventeen, when my best friend, Bugus, and I started to navigate this musical journey, we equipped ourselves mentally—besides being each other's biggest fans and best sounding boards, we also educated each other. We acquired a small arsenal of books that empowered us to stay positive, to build immunity to self-doubt, and to weather the years of waiting for the rest of the world to recognize what we already knew. I was never a big reader, which is why this whole venture is kind of hilarious to my family, especially to my brother, Frank, who seems to read a different book every day, but the books that I did read were instrumental in arming me with the mental artillery to succeed. I wanted to read them because they offered me something I could use. That's what I want this book to be for you—something you can use.

My confidence, or cockiness (whatever you want to call it), isn't fueled by a sense of superiority and it isn't based on my success. Yes, I believe I'm great, but I believed that when I was a kid making shitty music in my basement—that's how I got to where I am today. I'm successful because I am confident, not the other way around.

I want you to understand that I'm not shit. Truly. But the fact is that I always believed I was *the* shit, and that's the trick. Look at me and think, *If he believes in himself, then I can believe in myself, because who the fuck is he?* Look at me and know that you can absolutely do it. You can instill that insane confidence in yourself and get wherever it is you want to be. All my confidence and success should do is make you feel like you can be great too.

After eleven albums, ninety-six singles (I'm probably missing a few . . .), and ten years of sitting in a basement—literally and figuratively—I finally made it to the proverbial penthouse. Some of you might feel trapped in the basement. Some of you might be stuck on the third floor. Some of you might not even realize you're in an elevator. What I've laid out in these pages are tools you can use to fix your own elevator, or at least help you see that you are in an elevator, and then we can both celebrate in the penthouse and shoot through the ceiling of the whole place, because . . . THERE IS NO CEILING. It's all in your head.

PART 1

DELUSION

01

MANIFEST

SPEAK YOUR GOALS INTO EXISTENCE

YOUR THOUGHTS
HOLD WEIGHT
IN THE UNIVERSE.

A long time ago, this woman told me, "You have to be careful what you think about, because it comes true." You can think things into existence. You can speak things into existence. You can believe things into existence. This is manifesting.

Music is an intangible embodiment of ideas that can permeate a room in this beautiful harmony of emotion and sound. It can fill space and enter bodies and minds. It can transport people too. My body is certainly not in the room while you are listening to my songs, and yet I am. Making music is a kind of manifesting. To make music, you take nothing and turn it into something. When you walk into a studio, it is dead quiet; there is nothing going on. There aren't any chords. There aren't any drums. Yet, with your imagination, your work, and your belief, you can have a song that changes the world. That in and of itself is manifesting—albeit a little bit quicker ROI (return on investment) than manifesting an entire career, but the same rough concept.

All my success is a manifestation of what's been in my head since I was this scrawny, little seven-year-old kid standing on the fireplace hearth in our living room, clutching the notebook that I'd written my songs in and rapping my heart out as if I were onstage. Before I knew who I was, I knew *who I was*.

Manifesting isn't simply thinking that something is going to happen; it is encompassing that reality with your entire being. It is standing on a hearth and believing you're on the stage of an arena. It is sitting in your bedroom filling notebooks with songs and feeling in your soul that what you write will reach the masses. It is building your dream brick by brick until you have the great wall of YOU.

Put yourself into the life that you want. Close your eyes and surround yourself with whatever you are manifesting. Immerse yourself in that moment. More important than what it looks like, embrace what it *feels* like. Make yourself feel the pride and joy of walking into your new home. Imagine the thrill of answering the phone and being offered your dream opportunity. Can you feel your spirit heat up? Your cheeks aching from smiling? That warm electricity shooting up the back of your neck? Can you feel the irrepressible joy? Transmute those feelings into your work every day as you move toward what you want.

Feel the success so deeply that you genuinely believe it's going to happen tomorrow. If it doesn't happen tomorrow, believe it is going to happen the next day.

You can do this for anything—ambitious career dreams or the beach house you want to buy your mom. Imagine pulling up to that beach house. Feel the car turning down the street, feel the wind off the water, hear the palm trees, smell the ocean. Internalize the warm feeling that will spread through you. Feel the joy emanating from your mom. These visualizations are acts of absolute faith; they leave no room for doubt.

Of course, you have to be proactive and put in the work, but when you tap into your own potential winning is just natural.

———

In April of 2011, my best friend, Bugus, and I were in Atlanta. He was rapping and I was producing. He had this song called "Cali" and he wanted to shoot the video in California. So we went out there with our friend who was filming the video, and another friend who was hanging with us, and we crashed with Bugus's brother in his studio apartment. It was so small that he had a Murphy bed, which he'd fold down at night while the rest of us slept on the floor.

It was my first time in California, and we drove around LA and up the coast, north of the city. The whole time we were out there we kept saying, "Somehow we are going to get on MTV." We fully believed it. I told my parents, "When you see me on MTV, don't say I didn't tell you so." But we had no idea how to make that happen.

"

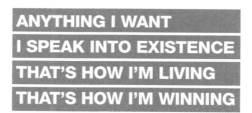

ANYTHING I WANT
I SPEAK INTO EXISTENCE
THAT'S HOW I'M LIVING
THAT'S HOW I'M WINNING

"

Yet, by October of that same year, we were on MTV. *Manifestation*. It was sheer force of will. We just kept poking away at the universe. Bugus was on Twitter harassing Rob Markman, who worked at MTV, just talking shit, which is what we always used to do to get attention. Finally, he checked our music out, and then BOOM he put us on MTV. We did an interview with Sway and Trina. That was the first big dream we manifested. This was the universe telling us we were on the right path. Bugus and I went back to the basement studio and worked our asses off.

For years I sat in my parents' basement, working all hours of the night and day. During the time I was down there making music that people didn't care about, I didn't hope or pray; I simply *believed* that my music was amazing and that I was *already* successful, though no one knew it yet.

While I was waiting, I got this jumbo-sized notepad and a red Sharpie and I scrawled out a bunch of signs and hung them around my room.

I HAVE A PLATINUM DEBUT ALBUM.
I AM THE BIGGEST ARTIST IN THE WORLD.
I'M THE MOST SOUGHT-OUT
PRODUCER IN THE WORLD.

I wanted to wake up surrounded by my goals. Back then I had to hype myself up. I wasn't merely hyping myself up on the surface; deep down I knew I was as great as I thought I was. But I was broke and had no results to coincide with what I felt; all I had were the thoughts in my head.

Those positive declarations weren't secret affirmations either. I posted them on Twitter, for the whole world to see—I was externalizing, which is part of the manifestation process. I wanted to document the "before" because I *knew* that I was going to make it. I wanted to be able to look back and say, "Yup, I knew it all along." Back in 2011, when I was still making shitty beats, I tweeted: "Million dollars a beat." My first Twitter handle was @RussOnTheBoards (that's what Bugus used to say right before every song), and then I changed it to @IMakeClassics. (Keep in mind this is before I ever made a song in my life. I was just producing for Bugus—though those songs are classic.) I was announcing to the universe what my dream was. I didn't just write those things; I lived and breathed and ate them. I believed them long before anyone started noticing my music. To me they were already true; in my head I'd already achieved my success. That's why most of those tweets and the notes on my wall were written in present tense.

People tend to talk about all the things that are going to happen in the future. They say, "I'm going to be successful, or I'm going to be a big artist." That's a mistake. When you set your achievement in the future, you are already putting it off. The future never comes. It will always remain the future, and you will always remain chasing it and waiting for it. You need to say, "I am successful." You need to believe that so deeply that you are just waiting for the world to catch up.

02

SINCE I WAS BROKE

BE DELUSIONAL

LIVING OFF DELUSION
IS HEALTHY.

Everything is unrealistic until it's not. Follow your dream despite its contradiction with the known reality and the rational expectations and assumptions of other people. You must believe in what you are doing before anyone else can.

If you feel you need advice or praise, you're the problem. If the fourteen-year-old me played me his music and asked for my honest reaction—though I would never have said this to him—would be, "This is terrible. I really don't see this working." But because I've been the fourteen-year-old with terrible beats *and* a twenty-six-year-old with a successful career, I know that if you're seeking outside validation, you are already losing to yourself.

You have to be delusional to even start, let alone to keep going. You have to be the first person who thinks that you're going to achieve what you have set out to do. When I was fourteen, contrary to the aforementioned hypothetical situation, I would never have asked the twenty-six-year-old me for advice, because I thought I was better than him.

When I was twenty-two, I would spend months at a time in a storefront basement owned by one of my good friends, Colm "KidSuper" Dillane. Despite being broke, sleeping on a couch that was too small even for me, and having questionable hygiene, it was my ideal situation—I got to sleep in a studio and focus on music 24/7. His store was a hub for up-and-coming artists. You never knew who would be passing through: a girl who made sunglasses for Lady Gaga, a redhead jeweler from Toronto, or a buzzing rapper from Brooklyn. One day around 5:00 p.m., my usual "morning," Colm came into the no-window cave of a studio that I was living in and woke me up to tell me that Joey Bada$$ was upstairs. Being in my position, it was exciting for me to be around people who had already made it. I was getting a snippet of a movie

"

**EVERYBODY IS A STAR
SOME JUST DON'T KNOW
HOW TO SHINE**

"

that I myself was still trying to create. I went upstairs, and he obviously had no idea who I was, but I didn't care. I was still getting a glimpse of success. We played keep-it-up with a soccer ball in the backyard. It was invigorating to see success still be able to be so simple.

Joey was my early indicator of how tangible the dream was. Without knowing it he fed my delusion. I easily could have met him and thought, *I'm still so far away.* Instead, I felt even closer to my dreams. In 2018 at my sold-out show at the Theater at Madison Square Garden, I brought Joey out to perform his hit single "Devastated." The delusion paid off.

That audacious self-confidence fed into everything else—it allowed me to put my work out into the world, it kept me striving to be heard, and it gave me the balls to think that on any given day I could wake up a star. That level of self-belief is the kind of insanity that is required to succeed.

Get Delusional.

03

THE FORMULA

YOU VS. YOU

EVERYONE NEEDS SOMETHING TO BELIEVE IN.

That thing should be *you* and what you COULD be if you just believe in yourself. We are all magicians—turning nothing into something is sheer magic. Despite popular opinion that you have to "see it to believe it," it's actually the opposite . . .

You have to *believe* it to see it.

The same things that make up stars make up us. We are all connected to the energy of a higher power so, in essence, having faith in the universe, or god, or whatever you want to call it is having faith in yourself and vice versa.

Self-belief is what makes you think you can run the race in the first place. However, to cross the finish line, you have to perform alchemy. You have to transmute that conjured belief into action.

What we fill our heads with holds real power.

Positive thoughts, affirmations, and a vivid, visceral feeling about what you want will put you on the wavelength to perform the magic trick: turning nothing into something.

The danger of having your dreams deferred lies in self-doubt. Dreams drowning in self-doubt will remain trapped on the ocean floor until your self-belief decides to rescue them. If what's in your head is negativity, you are tying cement blocks to your own feet. Doubt blooms like algae, and insecurity will lock you in your own cage.

You have the key.

I did this random show in Tampa in 2015. I was broke and couldn't afford to bring anyone but I was so excited just to be doing a show, let alone a show out of state. When I showed up to the hotel, the promoters, who were a couple, were extremely surprised to see that I was by myself. I checked into my room that was far from glamorous. I didn't care, I was just so excited that I was living inside one of

"

I'VE BEEN WRAPPED UP IN MYSELF
I'VE BEEN LIVING LIKE A MUMMY
SELF-BELIEF UNLOCKED THE DOOR
ON THE OTHER SIDE IS MONEY

"

–"The Formula"

my dreams that I asked them if they could get me a microphone and an audio interface. I was inspired. I needed to record.

I did the show and there were maybe forty people there, although forty felt like forty thousand. That moment was an embodiment of "happy to be here." Here, being inside the result of a manifestation. After the show, I went out with the fans and partied, but the whole time I was itching to get back to the hotel so I could record. I finally returned late at night to a studio setup, albeit bootleg, but it was enough. I made "The Formula" in that hotel room.

On the surface, none of this—the three-star hotel, the forty-person show, the bootleg studio, being broke—screamed success. Some people would even have been disappointed. However, inspiration is almost always found beneath the surface. The key to alchemy is finding beauty in the ugly.

CHAPTER

04

BOOMERANG

WHAT YOU THROW OUT WILL COME BACK

TRUST THE WHAT.
FUCK THE WHEN.

The come-up was way longer than I thought it was going to be. If you had told me when I was seventeen that nothing I did would blow up until I was twenty-three, or that at age twenty-six I still wouldn't have a Grammy, I simply wouldn't have believed you. I always thought it was going to happen tomorrow. But I loved the work so much that it wasn't work, and I lost track of time. I didn't have a routine; I didn't know whether it was Monday or Wednesday. Was the sun up or down? That was how I tracked the movement of time. Get so lost in your passion that the numbers on a clock aren't relevant. Time isn't real, just clocks.

Time is an obstacle you put in your own way. All you have to do is believe that it *is* going to happen. You can't put a deadline on success; you can't put a deadline on manifestation.

YOU MUST DETACH FROM THE WHEN.

You send things into the universe and they come back to you, but they don't always come when you expect or want them to. You have to know WHAT you want. If you are too attached to the WHEN, you will be fighting the natural flow of the universe. You may think you need a new job within the next three months, or that you need to launch your nonprofit by the end of the year, or that your greatest desire must be fulfilled *now*, but the universe already has the best plan. It knows the exact right moment everything needs to happen. That is not something you can control. Maybe you aren't as prepared as you think. Maybe the universe—which is a more informed version of yourself—wants you to develop your foundation before it gives you what you want. Maybe being delayed will mean that the market is more open or the economics will have shifted in your favor.

Don't get caught up in the WHEN.

Just know the WHAT.

"

**YOU'RE MY
BOOMERANG**

"

Never forget the WHY.

This ability to be flexible and maintain your belief is especially essential when your plans go awry. You have to bounce from failure to failure without losing enthusiasm. This trust allows you to be at peace and to freely throw your intentions into the world. Have faith that they will come back.

Trust the what. Fuck the when.

05

THE GAME

FUCK THE POINTS

FUCK THE POINTS, PLAY FOR THE LOVE OF THE GAME.

The game is your passion. Your passion is that thing that connects you to the truest version of yourself. Points are just the signifiers—the money, the accolades—and while they may be pleasurable, they don't sustain you. If you play for points, you will quit. The game is what keeps you going. You play it, simply for the sake of playing, because without it you are simply not living.

Stop trying to find love of life via money. That's backwards. It's just not going to work. You may find money, but you will still be miserable. You're going to find money through love of life. When you're chasing your dream, when you are so fulfilled by what you do that you're lost in the game, the money will find you.

First, find your passion. Start by answering one

question: What fills you up with the most enthusiasm when you think about it?

Almost everyone hesitates when asked that question. Did you?

I'm asking you: What fills you up with the most enthusiasm when you think about it?

That thing that popped into your head, that you dismissed just now because it isn't realistic—that was it. What was that?

If you don't know what your passion is, start where you find joy. Start following your curiosities. What do you do that uplifts your spirit? Whatever you are drawn to doing, you do for a reason. Explore that. But for most people, when they give an uncensored answer, their passion is evident. It's dance or drawing or starting a business. It doesn't matter what it is; it only matters that your enthusiasm is limitless and unbridled.

All too often people dismiss their own intuition. They dismiss it out of fear. They dismiss it because they've been told that there aren't enough jobs in that market or there isn't a lot of money. Limitations and boundaries are put on dreams by nonbelievers, quitters, and bitter people who didn't have the balls to go after their own dreams. FUCK THAT. Most people know what they really want to do; they just allow the poison that erupts from other people's pitfalls to convince themselves that they aren't talented enough, or that they don't love it enough, or that they can't do it because it hasn't been deemed credible, or practical, or lucrative.

Fuck those people. Get out of your own way.

Believe deeply in your passion. My passion is my religion. I mean that literally; I have a rosary tattooed on my arm—inside the prayer beads there are music notes. Music is my religion.

If you let your passion motivate you, the pursuit will become its own reward.

Don't worry about the money. Don't worry about the points. I know that there are bills to pay and mouths to feed and roofs to keep over heads, but if you're not down to struggle for an extended period of time, then you don't want it that bad. No job is beneath you. If working at McDonald's is what you need to do to keep your dream afloat, then that's what you've got to do. If you don't really want it that bad, then stop lying to everybody else and certainly stop lying to yourself. The truth is hard to swallow when you're choking on your pride.

Get lost in playing the game and stop worrying about the points. Points are just small tokens put there to distract and limit you.

If you play for the points, you will get rich and stop trying.

Play for the love of the game.

06

THE OTHERSIDE

**ON THE OTHERSIDE OF YOUR FEAR
IS YOUR TRUTH**

CONFIDENCE IS CONTAGIOUS AND AT THE SAME TIME OFFENSIVE. YOU PICK.

Have you ever seen a confident person get offended by someone else's confidence? No? Me neither. That's not a winning mentality. When you are consumed by your own passion, you are not focused on anyone else. That passion requires an insane level of self-confidence and a thick skin, because in order to succeed you have to believe in yourself more than the average person. And the average person is offended by that supreme confidence. You will piss people off. Accept that.

Pursuing your passion is the surest way to separate your true friends from the energy leeches— anyone who sucks the life out of you because they are too scared and self-loathing to go after their own dreams. But passion is also magnetic; it draws people together. The transfer of confidence that happens when you are around someone passionate is enlightenment.

We are often told that our dreams are unrealistic or that we need to make practical choices, but when you accomplish unrealistic goals, hell, even if you just fervently work at an unrealistic goal, it enlightens the people around you. It invites them to taste possibility. Your energy will inspire one another. Your successes will prove to one another what is possible.

My dad's family is filled with loud, shit-talking Italians who always had music going. His father, Pop Pop, played guitar for decades. The inception of my music-making career started in Florida when I would visit him and my grandmother. He always had his guitar with him and I was always fascinated to watch him play. It was just a matter of time before I picked it up and tried to play. He taught me a chord or two, and I was hooked. For my fourteenth birthday, he got me a guitar.

Our home was a comfortable place to pursue music. My parents always had music on—Earth, Wind & Fire or the Bee Gees—and they were always dancing. My dad would sing, add harmonies, go off on solos that weren't even in the song, and in the car he would turn the steering wheel into a drum set. I don't think my dad realizes how pivotal he was for me. His passion for music felt like my permission to pursue it. That's enlightenment.

"

> **YOU CAN PUSH A BUTTON**
> **AND SOMETHING POPS OUT**
> **ON THE OTHERSIDE**
> **BUT THEY DON'T TEACH THAT**
> **THEY JUST WANT YOU**
> **TRAPPED IN YOUR MIND**

"

In high school, the passion my friends and I felt for rap was infectious. I started out by making beats, and the guys who would rap would come to my basement to record.

Bugus would come to watch and assist, but pretty quickly the urge to make songs hit him, and then it hit me.

The domino effect happened. The contagious love for music started with Pop Pop, then went to my dad, who then passed it to me, and from there I brought it to school and shared it with my friends, specifically Bugus who then started pursuing his own passion, which circled back and inspired me.

I talk a lot about self-belief and NEVER doubting yourself, but I have to confess that there was a window in which I doubted whether I should, or even could, rap. At the end of 2010, I still thought of myself as solely a producer. I didn't believe in my voice, because I hadn't used it yet. I was sure it sounded stupid. At the same time, I'd always been writing. I'd written poems in high school; I'd help with certain flows and melodies in the studio while other people were recording. After a while, I gained confidence in my abilities as a writer and I started to think I should probably just start rapping. Then, one night, I was playing one of my beats for my brother, Frank, and I asked him, "Do you think I should start rapping?"

"Yeah, why not? I think you could do it." He was very supportive.

That conversation, along with my early thoughts of "I could do this," gave me the initial boost to start writing songs. I recorded them right on to my laptop—they sounded like dog shit, but I was just thrilled to be on the court. Then, almost a year after that conversation with Frank, I was down in Bugus's basement getting ready to record a hook on one of his songs.

While standing at the mic I suddenly stopped and let go of the wheel. Someone else had taken over. That someone was the elevated version of myself who was tired of being ignored. I turned around and asked Bugus, "Yo, should I start rapping?" Without hesitation he said, "Hell yeah! Do that shit!"

That was all I needed. I haven't looked back since.

Do you remember those first months after you got your license? Fun and freedom and wanting to always be driving? Endless possibilities? That's what it was like after I started making my own songs; it was invigorating and liberating. It was so new and I didn't want to do anything but that. The obsession had taken hold.

When somebody is confident and passionate, their enthusiasm is contagious. Bugus started rapping after he'd seen the other guys doing it. I started rapping after I watched Bugus doing it. The energy of the people you surround yourself with rubs off on you; choose wisely.

Fear is the wall. Belief is what catapults you over the wall.

Welcome to the otherside.

PART 2

PERSISTENCE

ALWAYS KNEW

HARD WORK > TALENT

YOU DON'T GET
DROPPED OFF
AT THE TOP
OF THE MOUNTAIN.

Dreams only work if you do. There's someone right now who wants what you want and is working harder than you. Work harder than everyone else. Don't fool yourself into believing you're not good enough, or that you are less talented than the next person. Get out of your way. I remember watching Kevin Durant get drafted into the NBA. He said: "Hard work beats talent when talent fails to work hard."

A lot of people think that talent is the essential ingredient to success. They're wrong. The X-factor is hard work. No one sees the hours Kobe spent in the gym or watching film on his opponents. They just see the final product—him scoring fifty over and over again. The reality is that the public will praise you for what you practice in private.

The reality is, if you love it, it won't feel like work. When you pursue your passion, the work you do will be a source of joy and fulfillment. The more you work, the more fulfilled; the more fulfilled, the better the work.

In school I had a shitty work ethic. I was one of those kids who didn't study and didn't do homework and would walk into class without realizing there was a test and still get an A or B. The work FELT like work. That was the problem.

I was a shitty employee too. Bugus and I worked at Outback Steakhouse as busboys (I only lasted a month). Next, this couple hired me to be a host at an Asian restaurant where my friend worked. I did everything from wait on tables to cook the vegetables, a job for which I was remarkably underqualified. One night it was raining really bad, the kind of rain where you drive with your hazards on, and my mom didn't want me to drive to work. I didn't complain because I didn't like the work. I spoke to my boss, the wife, and told her I couldn't come in, and they never put me back on the schedule. I didn't follow up because, once again, the work felt like work. I also worked at Off Broadway stacking shoes, when I was seventeen, the summer before leaving for college—a year and a half before I ever made my first song. We had these walkie-talkies that we used to communicate with the rest of the staff, and I would plug my headphones into my iPod and never know when one of the managers was trying to find me. But despite this lackluster track record, one of the reasons I am where I am in my life is because of my work ethic. When it came to music the work never felt like work.

I have worked on music all day every day since I was fourteen. Even when I'm not making music, I'm making music.

The summer assignment for my AP Psychology class in high school was to draw our "personality" vehicle. My classmates drew gondolas, bicycles, spaceships, etc.

I drew headphones.

I failed the assignment.

Headphones weren't a vehicle according to the teacher. But for me they were. Headphones, more specifically music, transported me to cities I'd never been, relationships I'd never had, and dreams that I hadn't actualized.

At fourteen, I had a friend named Alex who lived in my neighborhood. We would play guitar and write little melodramatic campfire songs. He had a keyboard and a drum set, and I would watch him play instruments and be inspired to learn them too. We used to sneak in to one of the equipment closets in the band room before school started, because that was where all the keyboards were kept. You could play any instrument on those keyboards, so that room was a place of free musical expression. It started to become a routine and we even amassed a huge crowd of three girls.

By the time I was a sophomore, I had discovered GarageBand on our family computer.

I felt like I had just gotten my license.

I started out by just putting a bunch of premade loops together. I probably made a thousand of those, and looking back, I realize that those were the infantile steps of learning how to structure a song.

Then I tried making my own beat. The first one was so, SO bad. I uploaded it to my YouTube channel one night and Frank asked, "What if you wake up tomorrow and have fifty thousand views?" (Fifty thousand was like fifty million—it was UNFATHOMABLE.)

I went to bed recognizing how far-fetched that seemed, but at the same time I was jittery, and could hardly sleep at the thought that that was ABSOLUTELY possible.

I woke up and it had fifty views.

Yet I felt the opposite of discouraged. I felt invigorated and motivated to try again. It became a challenge for me to blow up, and I wasn't going to stop until I did. It was in that moment that I realized that I DO have a work ethic; I just never had work that I loved.

Alex and I would meet in the neighborhood park and play our beats for each other and go fucking crazy. The other kids would be laughing and making fun of us, but we didn't give a fuck. We thought we were AMAZING.

Bugus found out we made beats, and he loved them. He hadn't started rapping yet, but he introduced us to a kid named Joe G who was. He would come over to our lunch table periodically and start rapping while providing his own beat via the table. If the journey is a staircase, the next stair had lit up. We needed to figure out how to record.

So we set up the most bootleg studio in my basement. We took the microphone from the video game *Rock Band* and duct-taped it to a guitar stand. We made a pop filter out of a wire hanger and pantyhose that my mom gave us, and then we put that in the closet and powered everything with the guitar amp, because it had a USB outlet so we could connect the microphone to the computer.

It was shitty, but it worked.

The first day that he came over we made a song. We were charged. If there was video of that moment, you would think we had won a Grammy.

We all went to school the next day and paraded the song around. We were our own street team. If you think I was excited about just making beats, you can imagine how excited I was to finally have a song *over* one of the beats.

Our crew's name was TSG—True Squad Generals. I made T-shirts for our senior class and handed them out from the back of my '97 Nissan after school while blasting our very mediocre songs. I loved what we were doing and believed in it every minute.

The crew dismantled shortly after its inception and all that was left was me and Bugus. We graduated high school and created DIEMON—Do It Everyday Music or Nothing—and that's what we did;

we made music every day. Together we formed a mastermind—when you and one other person come together and create a whole other force.

$1 + 1 = 3$

Upon the creation of DIEMON, we took on new members. Some of the guys put out a few songs; some of them put out one project; and some of them didn't even get to that point. In every case, when they didn't blow up instantly, they stopped. They were too attached to the idea of the *when*.

We would hype them up because we genuinely thought they were amazing, but they didn't have that core belief that kept them working, no matter how much we believed in them.

Picture self-belief as a cup.

My cup, along with Bugus's, was running over. We had enough to spare.

We would try to pour our belief into them before realizing our attempts were futile.

THEIR CUPS HAD HOLES IN THEM.

"

**ALWAYS KNEW I HAD
TO PUT IN WORK
ALWAYS KNEW THAT
THIS WAS GONNA WORK**

"

Eventually each of them faded out. Every once in a while, they cross my mind and I think, *You could've been HUGE*. Their talent was so evident. I was the last one to start rapping out of all my friends and I couldn't sing for shit . . . the fact that I made it and they didn't is as equally monumental as it is frustrating, because they were all better than me. One of the first ones to start rapping was older than us and he had the coolest voice. When he played us his first project I remember thinking, *This sounds so professional. This is what it is supposed to sound like*. I was in awe. He ended up stopping, and what I learned was that this world doesn't bet on talent. It bets on people who bet on themselves. The world rewards confidence and belief. Period.

You may be further along than me right now, or even have more talent, but I'm not gonna stop. I'm gonna out-work and out-believe you. That's how I got here.

08

PULL THE TRIGGER

DON'T HESITATE

JUMP OFF
THE FUCKING
CLIFF.

Embrace fear. It is natural to be hesitant when you're standing at the edge of the cliff and you know that in order to live a fulfilled life you have to jump. You're hesitant because you don't have wings . . . yet.

Pulling the trigger is about trusting your instincts. Your gut knows what you want to do before you do. Train yourself to listen to your first thought, the uncensored one.

Rash. Impulsive. Careless. Despite the negative connotations these are actually necessary components when it comes to mastering the art of pulling the trigger.

One of the earliest leaps of faith I took was dropping out of college. I hadn't even made my first song yet. I was solely dropping out to make beats and focus on production 24/7. The risk didn't resonate because I was more focused on jumping. I went to college after high school. I had straight A's, but shortly after midterms, my true calling could not be suppressed any longer and I lost interest in school. I missed one class, then I gradually started missing more and more, and then I stopped going altogether. While people were going to class, I stayed in my dorm room making beats and recording songs using nothing but my laptop. A part of me felt bad for not showing up to class until I realized that I already knew what I wanted to do with my life.

My mom was really upset that I didn't want to go to school. My whole life that's what she'd always wanted for us kids. My dad is the one who talked her off the ledge. He was super supportive of me pursuing my music. When they agreed to let me come home, my mom made me sign this piece of paper that basically said, that if I wasn't financially independent by such-and-such a date, then I'd have to go back to school or get a job. I signed the paper.

At the time, that date, which was, like, a year away, seemed so far off in the distant future. I thought, *Oh my god, by then I'm going to be an ultra-billionaire.*

That date came and went and I was still fucking nowhere. When I first uploaded my music on the digital music distribution platform, TuneCore, in 2011, on a good month I would make twenty dollars. Somehow I made it stretch. I would put five dollars in my gas tank. Bugus and I would throw in another five dollars each and get some disgusting alcohol. When we really wanted to treat ourselves, we would pool together another five dollars and get as many McDoubles as we could. Luckily, our moms were the MVPs, as most are. Mine being Italian, his being Nigerian, we never went hungry. That was my glamorous routine for five years.

I convinced my mom that I had to stay focused on my music. I was fortunate that my parents didn't make me pay rent; they're Italian . . . my mom would STILL prefer for me to live at home. Music was my day job and my moonlighting gig and my side hustle. I had finally jumped off the cliff and was in the middle of falling . . . but it felt like flying.

IT'S ALL IN YOUR HEAD.

"

I LOOKED UP AT THE SKY LONG ENOUGH I GREW WINGS.

"

–"MVP"

Looking back, even I think it was a nuts decision and a really ballsy one, but it wasn't intentionally ballsy. At the time I didn't think I was doing something brave. It was as if I was jumping off the cliff and it was so instinctual that I didn't even realize I was jumping off the cliff. In fact, I didn't see the cliff. I didn't even know I was jumping. If I'd been so hell-bent on the idea that there was a cliff and that I was going to have to jump off of it, then I probably wouldn't have jumped . . . I'm terrified of heights.

IT'S ALL IN YOUR HEAD.

The minute you think about something for too long, fear creeps in. You begin to doubt yourself. That's natural, however when you choose to be inspired by fear, you will actually end up flipping it into fuel and thriving off of it.

If you find yourself hesitating, don't.

The *what if* will torment you. The *oh, well* will free you.

Utilize that way of thinking continuously. The staircase of your dreams is daunting, because it is limitless and stretches far beyond what you can see. Stop focusing on the staircase and focus on the step in front of you.

Overcoming hesitation is an ongoing challenge that everyone faces. In moments of decision, don't hesitate. Less think, more do.

My intuition has driven my entire career—

whether it's quitting school or picking an album title or making business decisions. Back in 2014, two different labels reached out to me. They were very interested and I was very broke. Looking back, it is clear that making a deal then would not have been the best route for me. Easy to say now, but at the time, I was hardly making two hundred dollars a month. There was no reason not to sign, other than my intuition. The deals didn't feel right. I had developed such a strong connection with my intuition that the fact that it didn't *feel* right was enough for me. I had faith something better was coming.

"

I'D RATHER DEAL WITH OH WELL THAN WHAT IF.

"

–"I Want to Go Down with You"

Saying no to something that, on the surface, looks like a dream actualized takes a high level of intuition-influenced insanity. A record deal was a dream but this one felt like it could turn into a nightmare.

The offer was an acknowledgment from the universe that my work was not going unnoticed. Take those acknowledgments as little signs that you're on the right path. That is just the universe saying to you, "Keep going." It isn't saying, "This *is it.*"

If you approach offers and opportunities from a place of fear that they're the only ones on the way, then you've put a limit on what you can receive. Instead, appreciate that you and your work are being recognized and sought after. Let that awareness boost your trust in yourself.

Don't hesitate. Don't doubt. Don't even worry about falling. Wings *will* grow.

Jump.

"

PULL THE TRIGGER
AIN'T NOBODY
GONNA DO IT FOR YOU
PULL THE TRIGGER
DON'T HESITATE,
JUST SHOOT

"

09

NAKED

KEEP YOUR BARRIERS DOWN

VULNERABILITY IS A MAGNET.

My mom always tells me, "Keep your barriers down at all times." It is her way of reminding me to be open to receiving. It is a mantra that runs through my head all the time. What I've discovered is that keeping my barriers down doesn't just make me more receptive to inspiration, ideas, and success; it also allows me to be more vulnerable in my music and in my life. My mom gave me permission to be vulnerable.

Sensitivity and vulnerability get a bad rap, especially in the hip-hop world, where vulnerability can be perceived as weakness, even though it is a strength. People are very scared of facing their insecurities, let alone having them out in the open because they don't want those vulnerabilities to be used against them. What most people don't realize is that when you are honest about your vulnerabilities and when you wear them like a proud badge, then you block others from weaponizing your vulnerabilities against you. If you are upfront about your failings, your fears, your weaknesses, it is much harder to have them used against you. It is like Eminem's final battle in *8 Mile*, when he rapped about all the things the other guy was gonna make fun of him about so that when it was that guy's turn to go, he didn't have anything to say and he forfeited. Being honest with yourself and with others is the best way to disarm people.

I'm wildly honest. In personal relationships I'm such an open book. I'd rather you just know what's going on. I'm self-aware. You can't tell me anything about me that I don't already know or feel about myself, and if you did I'd probably say, "That's an interesting perspective." You can't use *me* against *me*. By being honest I flip my vulnerabilities into victories.

My career is an example of vulnerability winning. My first song to start gaining traction was "Goodbye." I put out the video in February of 2014. By December 6 of the same year it had become my first creation to cross the 100,000-view threshold. That was big for me, not just because I'd broken the 100,000-mark, but because the song was so personal. At its core it was a breakup song. The girl I was with had been unfaithful numerous times, so I made a song expressing my truth and included names of all those involved. I put myself out there fully and I was rewarded. That gave me a boost and confirmed the idea that vulnerability wins.

My songs are three minute autobiographies. That practice has taught me to freely bare my soul to the world. Instead of putting your best foot forward, put *all* your feet forward. This is it: take it or leave it.

The crowd favorite narrative is to not give a fuck about . . . anything. I give the most fucks. I care so much about my music and my life and my goals and that's part of why it has worked.

People always downplay how badly they want something so that if they end up not getting it they don't look stupid. Remember those kids in high school who would never let on how much they wanted to go to a particular college? They'd give some half-assed answer like "Yeah, I kind of want to get into that school" so that when they didn't get in they could plausibly say, "I didn't really want to go anyway." But if you really want to go to a particular college, to get a certain job, gain someone's love, or make your dream a reality, own that desire. What would happen if you wanted something unabashedly? If you had said your desire out loud you would have fought harder for it. At that point, you have to prove yourself right, which is far more powerful than proving someone else wrong. You are going to fall and it is going to look stupid to people on the outside, but what's even more stupid is being the people on the outside. They don't even believe in themselves enough to have the opportunity to fall. You have to be willing to throw yourself out there, and sometimes that means you will look foolish. Believe out loud.

I don't care about looking stupid. Actually that's a lie. In 2017, when I was already successful, I tweeted: "I can't wait to be at the Grammys next year I'm winning 10." Naturally, when the 2018 Grammys rolled around and I wasn't there, the internet had a field day. At first, I didn't feel foolish—I vocalized what I wanted to the universe without a timid-cross-your-fingers-yellow-apple-that-hovers-between-sweet-red-and-tart-green-kind-of-hope. But now I do have to confess that at a certain point that I did feel foolish and I deleted the tweet and I STILL don't have a fucking Grammy, so fuck y'all. Put my tweet back up.

In all seriousness this was a much-needed lesson in embracing my vulnerability. There are times throughout your journey when you have to check yourself and remind yourself of who you are. This was one of those moments.

If you are terrified of being critiqued, I suggest you do nothing and be nothing. That is the one way to avoid criticism, although you still won't be able to escape your own . . . and that's the only one that matters anyway. If you are living for the approval of others, you will always have a void. Fill the void with self-approval, which will blossom into self-love. People will try to tell you how to be you. They will tell you how and when to live, how to talk, how to dress, etc. Do not become a vending machine.

Don't give a fuck what anyone else says about you. Give more fucks about what you say about you. Yell out what you want and be honest about how badly you want it. Wear your heart on your sleeve . . . actually fuck the sleeves.

Get naked.

"

NOT YOUR BODY
I'M TALKIN' 'BOUT YOUR SOUL

"

10

THE STAKEOUT

PLOTTING WHILE BEING PATIENT

WATCH FILM
WELL BEFORE
YOU MAKE IT
TO THE LEAGUE.

At this point in this book you should already believe that you're in the league. Train like it.

Before I blew up, I was sitting in my little corner of the world. Nobody knew who I was. But I knew who they were. I was studying them every day and night while surveilling the music ecosystem so that I understood every minute detail.

When Bugus and I started making music, we covered the entire wall of his basement with magazine cutouts of rappers and various music-industry icons. It was a stakeout. If you went down there you would've thought we were solving a murder, or plotting one. It was our war room. We studied everything and everyone at play from interviews to show footage to underground songs and moments that the rest of the world was oblivious to. I consciously soaked up so much, and I subconsciously soaked up even more. Bugus and I studied the fan, the player, the coach, and the owners.

We knew every artist's discography inside and out. We knew which songs and albums fans responded to the most. We knew who actually owned the songs and albums. We knew who set up the tours for those songs and albums. You can't expect to succeed if you don't know what worked and what didn't work for people before you.

Back when I was nineteen, I thought everything Bugus and I were doing was going to blow up tomorrow. When it didn't, I had to learn that I could control my work and my self-belief, but not the timing. Patience was essential. I put out my first project in 2011, but it wasn't until the top of 2016 when things really started to take off. In that window of time I released eleven projects and more than eighty songs.

I thought my first project should instantly make me the biggest artist in the world, and when it didn't I was appalled: *How did it not blow up? What the fuck?* (When my music finally did take off years after that, I was thankful that it hadn't happened when I thought I wanted it to. Mentally I wasn't ready.)

Patience isn't just the process of waiting. It is your attitude and how you handle the waiting time.

Until my music took off, it was just trial and error. I fell on my face a bunch of times. I'd think something was going to blow up and then it wouldn't. When that happens ten times it would literally be insane to not think, *Alright, it might be something I'm doing.*

It was on project eight or nine that I really started to feel like I'd found myself sonically. Still, nothing had worked. When nothing works keep working.

I never lost an ounce of enthusiasm. I lost track of time. That's where I found success.

Have tunnel vision on a goal and keep your head down. Don't distract yourself and disrupt your

"

> ## PATIENCE TASTES BITTER, BUT THE AFTERTASTE IS SO SWEET.

"

–"Manifest"

momentum with the constant need to look up and look around. You have to master the balance of awareness and focus. You'll know when to look up.

When I put out projects nine, ten, and eleven, I knew that they were great, and I couldn't understand why they weren't working. So I came up with a new strategy of putting out a song a week. I had studied that when dropping an album, more times than not, the song with the most amount of plays was the first one on the album. I reflected on my career up until that point and realized that the music was not the

"

I BEEN CALCULATIN',
LIVIN' IN THIS HOUSE
OF PATIENCE
QUARANTINED MYSELF

DOWN HERE,
BUT NOW
I'M BREAKIN' OUT
THE BASEMENT

"

issue, the delivery of it was. I had an epiphany that I should essentially drop one-song albums. Every song would get its own promotion, its own artwork, and its own fair chance at being heard.

I went away for a couple of months and just made a bunch of songs. I wanted twenty-six songs in the vault because I knew that being half a year ahead would provide me with more than enough cushion to create without conflict. I also made my whole next album, because I KNEW I was going to blow up and I didn't want to have to scramble and make an album on the fly once it happened. Chess, not checkers. I knew what my next move was going to be, and I had a plan for how to play the entire game. Once I had half a year mapped out, then I put out song one. I wanted to always be six months ahead so that *when* everything took off and I couldn't get into the studio as often, I'd still have music to release. I spent that time painting a perfect sonic portrait of myself.

At that point the whole world was telling me it's

not going to work. I had journalists telling me it's not going to work. My own career results were telling me it was not going to work. I had put out eleven fucking projects and nothing had taken off. The takeaway from all of this though was that I was now highly versed in what didn't work. I studied my failures and strategized my triumphs. The delusion at the beginning of my career was now backed by research. *Let me try one more thing—the song a week until I blow up.* It worked. My TuneCore earnings crept up and then they skyrocketed. In June 2015 I made $620, and in June 2016 I made $102,000.

Keep going consistently and positively, and if it doesn't work out, then pivot, switch your approach, and keep going.

Never stop studying.

11

DO IT MYSELF

HOW TO SURVIVE IN THE WILD

YOUR LIFE IS ON THE LINE. YOU SHOULD BE THE ONE TAKING THE SHOT.

Self-sufficiency is a powerful freedom, one you grant to yourself. Try everything. Throw away the manual. Give yourself the education on how to survive in the wild.

Knowing that you are enough is invigorating. When you succeed on your terms and only your terms with no one else's fingerprints on your work you become a superhero. There is nothing you can't do at that point.

Captain your own ship. How are you going to build a ship, let someone else steer it, and then be surprised when it doesn't go in the direction that you had in mind? Or worse: Why would you abandon your own ship in the first place? Artists often sign deals that do exactly that, deals that have them ceding control of their creation. Stay in the cockpit.

People often get rid of their entire ship when they get offered another one. Or, even more tragic some people barely even have a ship—they are still putting their little raft together on the sand when some big, shiny ship pulls up and offers them a ride, and due to a lack of self-belief and confidence that the little thing they're building is going to turn into a big, shiny ship one day, they board the better-looking alternative. But you never really know who or what you'll find on that big ship, and you may not like how it's being run and where it's headed, and you might end up wishing you were back on your own ship, boat, or raft on the sand.

Even if you take your ideas, your talent, or your art to a larger entity, navigate that choice on your own terms. If you decide to get on someone else's ship just make sure yours comes along too, so that you always have an *out* . . . which is really just an *in* back to yourself.

Too many people, especially creative people, shy away from the business side of their careers. They are scared of what they don't understand and feel like it is not their job to understand. In too many cases, that results in them relinquishing those responsibilities to others. Oftentimes this leads to mismanagement of their career and causes turmoil that unfortunately leads to their self-inflicted demise.

Educate yourself. You have to be hands-on with your dream if you want it to go your way. The business side should support the creativity, not control it, and certainly not interfere with it.

No matter what you do, the deeper your understanding of the full scope of your career—from creative to sales to the mechanics—the better equipped you will be to survive in the wild.

I have always questioned authority. I questioned teachers. I questioned principals and the principles. I questioned managers. I questioned bosses. Having a boss was never for me. The idea of someone else

"

> ## THE DAY I LET SOMEONE ELSE BECOME THE BOSS OF ME WHEN THERE'S A BOSS IN ME, I'LL BE DAMNED

"

–"What They Want"

ever having the power to tell me what to do, let alone contractually, wasn't for me. I didn't have to know the ins and outs of the business to know that I didn't want a boss. I didn't want to give up control of the what, how, when, and why I was making what I was making.

For me, the first step in self-sufficiency was owning the means of operation. I wanted uninhibited freedom to self-explore sonically. That type of self-exploration requires a forum that doesn't have curfews and random passersby. From the extremely

"

I DON'T NEED HER,
I DON'T NEED HIM,
FUCK IT,
I'LL DO IT MYSELF

"

bootlegged studio in my parents' basement to the upgraded studio in Bugus's parents' basement, we always intuitively knew that we needed to own the gym we were practicing in. The lights were always on.

Self-reliance is purely a survival technique. I didn't have a choice. I wanted to make a song but I didn't know how to do it, and I didn't know anyone who did. I couldn't call anyone. I had to figure it out, from the producing to the writing to the engineering to the performing to the mixing to the mastering. Those titles were irrelevant to me and still are. I had one goal—make a song. Any role that I had to play to complete the song I did instinctively. So I just banged on buttons till it sounded good.

When I produced Bugus's first two projects, we still thought of the mixing of a record as this foreign thing that we needed someone else to do for us. I didn't even really know what it was or what it entailed. So back in 2010, during our second semester of our senior year in high school, when we could still afford him, Bugus found this guy on Twitter, MixedByAli, who was the in-house mixer for, at the time, a very underground independent LA label called Top Dawg Entertainment. (He is now a Grammy-winning mixer who has worked with everyone from Drake to Dr. Dre.) We would send him stuff to mix and then he would send it back. But sometimes the mixes didn't sound the way we had imagined. Eventually, I said, "You know what, we know what we want it to sound like, so let's just do it ourselves." I started consciously putting on the mixing hat, clicking and pressing buttons until I found combinations that sounded like what was in my head.

What I learned was that by doing it myself I got the sound I wanted. It's that simple; no one knew what I wanted my music to sound like more than I did, so if I could just figure out how to make the connection between the sound I heard in my head and the sound coming out of the speakers then I knew we were fine.

I was working on several careers at once. I was trying to perfect making beats. I was trying to perfect being a writer. I was trying to perfect being a rapper and singer. I was trying to learn how to perform, engineer, mix, and master. Trial and error was the best teacher I ever had. Self-sufficiency was why I was able to make so much music—because I didn't have to call anyone. I could go downstairs and make a whole album and not have to pick up the phone once. That was freedom. Freedom is power.

Music is collaborative, and beautiful things happen when you work with other musicians, but you don't want to be in a position where you are dependent on anyone else to make a song.

I need to be productive. I'm impulsive. I need to be able to create at any moment. I don't have time to ask someone else to facilitate my creativity. *Get out of the chair and I'll do it!* I was controlling my own workload, controlling my own growth, and therefore controlling my own trajectory.

When you put on each hat and you try out each different line of work, no one can bullshit you anymore, because you have gotten your feet wet in every craft's pond. When we started shooting music videos, we had our friend who was really talented at making them helping us, but he would take a really long time. We just figured it was taking as long as it was supposed to, because that's what he said. We didn't know any better. We didn't know what goes into it. And then we got sick of waiting for him, so

"

HELD THE CAMERA ONCE OR TWICE AND I EDITED TOO WHEN I SPEAK IT'S FROM EXPERIENCE OF EVERY SHOE

"

−2006

Bugus and I went and got a camera and we thought, *How hard can this be? Just press record.* Then, we bootlegged the Final Cut Pro software so we could edit our footage. We went to LA and shot a video for "Goodbye." The very next day, I edited the video and then we put it out. (Now it has over ninety million views on YouTube. It is RIAA–Gold Certified.) Our friend had been telling us that this was a month-and-a-half project, but we turned it around in two days. Once we figured out that aspect, Bugus and I went to a photo studio and shot six videos in one day. It only takes a long time when other people do it. It doesn't take a month and a half to turn around a music video. It takes a month and a half for them to get around to it because they don't love it like you do.

Don't fall asleep on yourself. YOU are the answer.

12

DON'T FALL FOR IT

ANTI-DOGMA

BUILD
YOUR OWN
REALITY.

Society sets you on a path toward a "dependable," predictable life-in-a-box. The path to college. The road to success. The way to happiness. A lot of people will tell you that what you want to achieve can't be done. Never internalize their limits as your own. Don't fall for it. There is no one-size-fits-all path. To figure out what you want and how to get it, you must follow your own path. To certain onlookers you might appear lost. You are not lost. You are exploring.

Society wants your life itemized in boxes that they can put labels on. They want you to behave a certain way. They want you to follow a certain career path. They want you to date a certain person. You must recognize this and reject it. Life truly starts on the outside of the walls. Don't fall for the idea that you need a relationship to be happy. Don't fall for the idea that you need to be realistic or humble or practical. Don't fall for your own doubt and don't fall into the trap of comparison. Your mirror should only show one reflection.

It is easy, natural, and encouraged to feel on top of the world when you reach any milestone in your career, no matter how big or small. A lot of upcoming artists lose to themselves in the arena of comparison. The 10,000 plays that can make you feel as tall as a skyscraper are the same 10,000 plays that can make you feel as small as an ant. The variable is that you took your eyes off your own grass and checked how much greener everyone else's was. Naturally, you saw several lawns that appeared greener than your own, which ultimately fueled your sense of inferiority. The reality is that you may think that someone's grass is greener than yours, but they might have AstroTurf.

When you lose yourself in something you are passionate about, you will find yourself there too. But in order to lose yourself, let alone find yourself, you will need uninterrupted *time* by yourself.

You must work in the dark for your light to shine. Being alone is imperative. It's when you're going to self-explore. If you are constantly seeking company then you need to take a step back and reassess. You are scared to face yourself. Embrace this fear and take it on as a challenge. Take it day by day. This is a race, yes, but not against anyone or anything else except your own doubt.

A lot of people get alone and think, *I'm lonely.* So many people define and limit their lives to wanting a relationship above all else. So, instead of choosing a person out of love, they choose a relationship out of fear of being alone. They are trying to fall in love with someone else before they fall in love with themselves. This will never work; you will always have a void that only you can fill. You will find the person you are supposed to find when you are living your true purpose—in fact, you will both actually *collide* into each other. Don't set relationship goals. Set life goals. If people worked toward their dreams with the same zeal that they worked toward getting into a relationship they would be successful.

I'm not saying stop putting love first. I'm saying stop misplacing love. Start by putting that love into yourself. Fall in love with a dream of yours. This type of self-love only grows in the garden of solitude.

When I was alone, music happened . . . I happened. Music is my best friend and my passion. It is who I wanted to spend time with.

One afternoon in high school, I was at the piano talking with my music theory teacher, Mr. Spraggins, about whether to go to school for music or whether I should do something more "practical." I didn't mean it. I was regurgitating what I'd heard from my parents and society:

"I don't want to put all my eggs in one basket and just go do music."

"Just make sure you have a basket," he said.

Fireworks shot across my brain. Everything in my soul shifted. Here was this teacher who I only had for one semester in high school, providing me with life-changing advice. I've known people for much longer who have impacted my life far less. Don't block your blessings because you are so crippled by the idea of where the message should come from that you fail to receive the message. He didn't want me to fall in the trap of playing it safe. He didn't want me to fall in the trap of doing what my parents wanted me to do—my mom wanted me to be a lawyer or a finance guy (I once won the school-wide stock market game). He didn't want me to fall for being realistic.

"Be realistic" is the worst advice I've ever received. It is a commonly used phrase that, when internalized and accepted, brands a life of mediocrity.

The people championing realism are usually the people who gave up on their own dreams. The reason someone will tell you something is unrealistic is because you haven't done it yet, and deeper than that, THEY themselves haven't done it yet. Being realistic is claustrophobic. It suffocates you and limits you to only what's been done so far. Will Smith explained in an interview: "It is unrealistic to walk into a room and flip a switch and lights come on. Fortunately, Edison didn't think so. It is unrealistic to think that you can bend a piece of metal and fly people over an ocean. That's unrealistic."

I moved around a bit as a kid—New Jersey, Kentucky, North Carolina, and Georgia. Doing that can either make you get heavily attached to things or provide you with a sense of detachment, because you see that certain things and people are interchangeable. I think for myself it was probably a little bit of both. I wasn't that close with the other kids so all I had was myself. That social detachment freed me. It freed me to be alone with myself. I became centered, which is something I've been able to carry with me throughout my journey. It is a source of confidence and pride. It has given me immunity to certain social constructs.

Individual thinker > Group thinker.

I hate the word *humble* with a vengeance. The dictionary definition is disappointing to say the least given how idolized the character trait is. The word *humble* has been defined as to be marked by modesty or meekness with regard to spirit or attitude or behavior, or as showing submissive respect, being low in rank or quality. All of these things are about lowering yourself to appease others. I understand what people are trying to say; they're trying to tell you to stay grounded. But you can be grounded without being weak in behavior or low in rank, and you should not pretend that you are a part of some strange show for other people where whoever has the most curtailed confidence wins.

Being humble is living according to other people. Because even that humble person thinks they're the greatest thing in the world. But in order to come off humble, in order to not offend insecure people, they will silence their roar. Society doesn't feel comfortable unless you are wearing a muzzle. No one who is winning has a problem with someone else winning. Being humble is a strange societal rule that has been drawn up to keep your own confidence in check and keep your self-belief in their pocket. They want to decide when you can have your own confidence. Humility makes you your own worst enemy. Why spend time trying to dim your own light out of fear that it could get in someone else's eyes? If their light was shining, they wouldn't even see yours.

There are always going to be people who do what they're told, who play it safe, who follow the rules, and who criticize anyone who doesn't. There will also always be people who question, who take risks, who embrace uncertainty, and who are open to discovery. Which kind of person do you want to be?

Don't fall for it.

13

EMERGENCY

MOVE WITH A PURPOSE

LIVE IN
A STATE OF
URGENCY.

When I was a kid my mom always said, "Move with a purpose." If I was upstairs and she called my name, she'd be furious if I said, "What?"

"If I'm calling you it means move with a purpose," she'd tell me sternly.

That is ingrained in my head. Move with a purpose. Move with urgency. Move like you're trying to make it happen by tonight, like there is someone else out there in their basement working super hard who is going to take it away from you if you don't do it first.

People are too noncommittal to their dreams. "I'll get to it," they say. They're always putting things off. When I ask people about their goals, their end game, I often hear, "Well, for right now I'm doing this, but later on . . ." Stop waiting. There is no later on.

Nothing is going to change between now and then unless you do. Putting something off until later is a sure-fire way to never do it.

My dad used to hold us kids accountable in that regard, whether it was homework, chores, or prepping for the game. We would often say, "Yea, don't worry. I'll do it later." He would instantly retort with, "I'll do it *when?!*" and then he'd answer himself, "I'll do it NOW."

People use the future as an excuse to procrastinate. Treat your life like it's a ticking time bomb . . . because it is. Time is our most prized possession.

Some people don't understand the value of a dollar, but far worse than that is that even more people don't understand the value of a minute. It took me forty-five minutes to make "What They Want," a now RIAA Double-Platinum certified song (might be Triple-Platinum by the time this book comes out). This was also one of the first songs that catapulted my career. It changed my life. I understand the value of a minute, let alone forty-five.

When you understand that time is the one thing you can't get back, you will spend it wisely. A lot of people, however, are just going through the motions and don't even notice the time passing. You will encounter a lot of these types of people along your journey, oftentimes in the form of a relationship.

Some women I've tried to get to know have questioned how serious I am about them because I wasn't giving them the traditional indicators of affection—good morning texts, "gifts," et cetera. I was surprised because I was giving them the most precious gift I had: my time. Spending forty-five minutes on the phone, even if it is just once a week is a big deal to me, because I know that forty-five minutes in the studio can impact the world and my lineage long after I'm gone.

If you're dealing with someone who doesn't understand the value of their own time, then they

"

YOU KNOW
I'M ALWAYS MOVING
WITH A SENSE
OF URGENCY

"

certainly will not value yours. They will dismiss the real and idolize the fake.

Time > flowers.

There is always something to be done. As long as you are accomplishing one small facet of the bigger picture every day then you are spending your time wisely. Don't worry about being perfect. Be more concerned with being productive. Think less. Do more.

Overthinking can paralyze your progress. Get out of your way. I've said a lot about the power of thought, of putting what you want into the universe and believing in yourself, and filling your head with the ideas that can propel you forward. But in the end, all of those thoughts are useless if it isn't compounded into action. You can think you are the greatest, but if you don't do anything, no one will ever know.

Keep doing. Keep making. Keep pushing. It's about output. Do it so you can do it again. Get in as many reps as possible. Repetition is the father of perfection. You have to simultaneously believe that what you are doing is good and have the foresight to understand that even if it is not as good as you want, it will become great through practice. You have to be okay with not being great for a year or ten. Even when you've reached your first goal, when your belief has finally been recognized and manifested in the universe, your work will not be perfect. Perfection lives on the horizon; it is elusive. You will keep leveling up and keep chasing perfection. You will continuously strive to be the best version of yourself—there is always more to do.

Move with a purpose.

PART 3

GRATITUDE

14

TAKE IT ALL IN

THE TORNADO EFFECT

I CREATED
THE STORM.
I KNEW IT
WAS COMING.

The tornado effect is when you know a tornado is coming—the weather forecasters have announced that a storm will hit, the governor has told all citizens to take shelter, and you have found safety down in the basement. You have listened as the wind uprooted trees and knocked debris against the house—but still, after the storm, you emerge from the basement and stare at the aftermath in awe. You are blown away that it actually happened, even though you'd not only expected it to happen but prepared for it. You knew that your dreams were going to manifest.

You weren't surprised that the storm actually hit, but that doesn't take away from the magnitude of the aftermath.

That's what it is like when your success finally hits. Even though you have manifested your success and spent years believing it was inevitable, the reality of it can still inspire awe. It is essential to recognize your achievements and to feel gratitude for your wins, large and small. Gratitude is your way of telling the universe, "Thank you, I'll have some more."

If you're not grateful for the blessings you currently have, what makes you think you're going to receive more?

Celebrate what you want to see more of.

"

I WENT FROM NOTHIN'
TO SOMETHIN' GUESS
I DONE CAME A LONG
WAY I CAN'T STOP NOW

I'M ALWAYS WORKIN' I KNOW
DEEP DOWN THAT I'M
DESERVING OF WHAT I GOT
OF WHAT I'LL GET

"

15

POTENTIAL

LOOK UP TO YOURSELF

THE FUTURE VERSION OF YOURSELF SHOULD BE YOUR INSPIRATION.

Get obsessed with the idea of a better you. The process of getting better is the fun part. That's why I keep working. That's everything. The idea that there is always an upgraded version of myself that can be attained is what keeps me going. I'm often asked about which artists inspire me. The answer is "the future me." I'm aware that that sounds arrogant, and, of course, I listen to and am moved by and excited by a lot of great artists. But when it comes to inspiration, my biggest motivator is my own potential.

Consider your life as a video game—you create a player, start out as a 60 overall, pick your position, and navigate your career accordingly. What keeps you playing the game is the tangible possibility of becoming a 99.

Stop looking up to other people, even to me. I'm not shit. When your number one driving factor is your potential, then your success starts and ends with you. It is all in your head.

Your potential has no roof. Stop giving it ceilings. My mom is a certified life coach. She's super intuitive and very spiritual. One of my favorite things she always says is, "What if it can turn out better than you can imagine?"

Maybe you only believe your boutique can be a local shop rather than envisioning a national chain. Or you see your startup doubling in its first year,

"

I GET MY INSPIRATION FROM MY OWN POTENTIAL.

"

—Lapped

"

I KNOW WHAT YOU COULD BE
I KNOW WHAT YOU SHOULD BE
I JUST HOPE YOU WAKE UP

"

which sounds like an enormous amount when you are at zero, but what if it can turn out even better than that? Or you think you can only get a million-dollar record deal, but what if you could get a two- or five- or ten-million dollar deal? Why cap it at one? Don't stop yourself from becoming a 99 just because you think you're only a 60.

As long as you are becoming the best version of you, you will not disappoint yourself. If you ever have a crisis of faith, you will always have the answer: **The answer is YOU.**

CHAPTER

16

THE JOURNEY

SUCCESS IS NOT A FINAL DESTINATION

THE DREAM
IS LIVING IT.

Too many people are waiting to arrive at success. They are suspending their happiness and fulfillment until they arrive at a destination that doesn't exist. The journey is the success.

Trust the process. As long as you stay on your path and know where you're headed, you have to accept that any obstacle along the way is exactly where it is supposed to be. Let the world go and watch it all come to you, or fight it till the end and watch what it does to you. You choose.

Blind faith is your compass.

Imagine being lost and blindfolded and someone coming up to you and telling you to just follow them. You oblige. You can't see where they are taking you, but you recognize the voice. It is your own.

You know the way.

When I was fifteen my dad told me, "You don't know how to be content. You'll get twenty Grammys and be pissed that you didn't get twenty-one." He's right. I'm terrified of being content. I could go make my favorite song I've ever made tonight, and I will absolutely be satisfied and in love with it, but by the time the song is finished, I am already hooked on the idea of making a better one.

Each "favorite" song I make doesn't make me stop. I don't think to myself, "Okay, that's it, I did it. I can retire." They are simply celebrations of the never-ending journey.

Until you die there is always a road that you haven't been down yet.

A fan gave me a ukulele, and even though I don't play ukulele, I wrote two songs on it ("No Matter What" and "99"). Like John Lennon said: "I'm an artist, and if you give me a tuba, I'll bring you something out of it." The thrill of the journey is embracing newness as long as it is in sync with your purpose.

"

THERE AIN'T NO
DESTINATION MAN . . .
THE JOURNEY
IS EVERYTHING

"

It's impossible to know exactly what's going to happen along the way—who you are going to meet, where, when. . . . Uncertainty is a wild card that should be used as fuel.

Blowing up at nineteen is the greatest thing that never happened to me. At that time I thought my journey was much shorter than it ended up being, much shorter. The journey is forever.

Your car will never stop and when it does, you won't even be around to see it parked.

Just enjoy the ride.

17

BACK TO LIFE

BOUNCE BACK

YOU *WILL* FALL.

The reality is that this isn't easy. It is not supposed to be. A certain amount of struggle is necessary in order to appreciate success.

They will try to break you. But, God forbid it happens, breakdowns create breakthroughs.

I went through a phase in 2018 where I was not at peace. I let the chaos that my life had become drag me down into the depths of darkness. Suddenly, this perception of me was being formed and an insane amount of negativity was being cast onto me. Rather than letting go and accepting that this was all part of my journey, I was trying to fight it. I was sick of the vitriolic lies. Hate I could handle, but lies about me, lies that even some of my own fans that I had worked so hard to get, believe, drove me crazy. I was in a dark place and I felt hopeless.

I needed a break from the madness. The journey up until that point was me versus me. I turned it into me versus the world. I was losing an imaginary battle. It is always you versus you.

Life is one big fucking contradiction. I'm sitting here telling you that *it's* all in your head, and yet I was losing to the thoughts in my head. However, in the middle of adversity is where you discover who you truly are.

For a second, I got lost. I forgot the very tools that got me here in the first place. I had to step back and tell myself to relax and remind myself that I couldn't control all this shit; what I could control were my thoughts, what I put out into the world, and my behavior. I decided to trust that whatever happens is actually what is supposed to happen. I realized that this was all just part of my journey and that it was going to contribute to making everything that much better in the long run. Besides, I don't want some smooth-sailing career. Smooth seas do not make skillful sailors.

I deleted social media off my phone for a month

and a half. (I planned on taking a much longer break.) I told everyone that I wasn't touring. I didn't want to do any interviews. I had to reconnect to myself. Of course, on day one and a half, I was making a song. Music is my therapist. I also had time to focus on the "small" things that are actually the big things—my family and my friends. I put all of my feelings and experience back into my craft rather than harboring them and giving them the power to keep me down. I snapped out of it so that I could snap back into it—it being the dream life that I had created.

When you are down and you rise up, you feel more powerful than you ever did. On the other side of adversity is strength.

"

I COME BACK TO LIFE THEY
TRYNA KILL ME WITH THEIR
WORDS BUT THAT AIN'T GONNA
WORK, NO I COME BACK TO LIFE
SOMEBODY LET THEM KNOW
THEY MIGHT HAVE GOTTEN
CLOSE BUT I COME BACK TO LIFE,
YEA

"

KEEP ON GOIN

MAIN FOCUS IS TO STAY FOCUSED

THE JOURNEY STARTS AND ENDS WITH YOU.

Keep the faith.

"

HAVEN'T SLEPT
SINCE '06

"

Acknowledgments

First and foremost, I would like to thank myself.